£1·50

IMAGES OF
CAMBRIDGE

IMAGES OF
CAMBRIDGE

compiled by
Michael J. Petty MBE

breedon **books**
PUBLISHING

First published in Great Britain by
The Breedon Books Publishing Company Limited
44 Friar Gate, Derby, DE1 1DA.
1994, reprinted 2006.

© Cambridge Newspapers Limited

ISBN 1 85983 546 5

Printed and bound by Cromwell Press, Trowbridge, Wiltshire.

Contents

Introduction

CAMBRIDGE is a relatively small East Anglian town. It is also a world city, with a massive reputation built on its ancient university, pioneering hospital and, more recently, its fast-growing high-tech industrial sector.

It is a tribute to the skill and dedication of Michael Petty that this book brings the city to life through pictures. His enthusiasm for his subject, which knows no bounds, is infectious.

We are indebted to him, the staff of our promotions and photographic departments and our library, and to all those who have played a part in the publication of this splendid book.

Robert Satchwell
Editor
Cambridge Evening News
September 1994

Foreword

WHY add yet another title to the heaps of books on Cambridge?

Perhaps because there are at least two Cambridges. One the visitors do not see and the other that residents can only glimpse. And both have changed dramatically since 1900.

In 'Images of Cambridge' they come together but with more emphasis on East Road than West Road, more on King's Hedges than King's Parade and more on the modern Elizabethan than on the Edwardian Age.

I have tried to chart developments as they happened throughout the twentieth century, decade by decade.

Within the town there are essential issues of house building and slum clearance, the growth of the Arbury estate, changing shopping patterns with small shops making way for Lion Yard, Grafton Centre and Grand Arcade. And then there is traffic – the terror of Mitcham's Corner by day and night, the coming of Elizabeth Way, which solved the problems for a short while, and the Green Bikes which did not.

Within the university gowns give way to women undergraduates, Greek and Latin to Management Studies, new colleges and new ways of enjoying academic life.

Sometimes the two worlds conflict as when the Rag was disrupted by town yobs but at others they come together when May Ball revellers queued for breakfast outside a cafe in the Kite Area.

Its chronological arrangement makes it possible for the reader to see Cambridge as they first knew it, either as a child in the 1920s, as an undergraduate in the 1950s or a citizen in the 1980s. You may also see yourself, for the streets are full of people in the dress of the time and the cars of the period. You can then see how and when the change occurred, or turn back the pages to discover what had already happened in previous decades.

Bringing together photographs from a wide range of sources I have drawn extensively upon both the files of the *Cambridge Evening News* and those of the Cambridgeshire Collection at the Central Library in Lion Yard. With action photographs, formal groups and family snapshots, they represent some of the work of the city's top professional and amateur cameramen including H.S Johnson, Percy North, Harold Culpan and John Scoon as well as members of the Cambridge Antiquarian Society.

For their assistance in locating the pictures chosen I gratefully acknowledge the assistance of the staff of the *Cambridge Evening News,* Cambridge & County Folk Museum, the Librarian of the Cambridge Antiquarian Society and my former long-suffering colleagues in the Cambridgeshire Collection.

Inevitably something will have been missed and such omissions are mine, but they can be filled by the assistance of those who notice them. The Cambridgeshire Collection welcomes additional pictures that may be shared with future researchers. Likewise prints of virtually everything contained within these covers can be supplied to anybody who does indeed find some image of Cambridge which catches their interest.

Mike Petty, September 2006.

The 1900s

The death of Queen Victoria in 1901 marked the end of an era. Victoria had visited Cambridge on two occasions, once to see her beloved husband, Prince Albert, made Chancellor of the university in 1847. He had been responsible for many of the reforms which brought science into the forefront of its teaching and research. Their son and heir, the Prince of Wales, the future King Edward VII, had attended university for one term, using Madingley Hall as his residence, and causing considerable newspaper comment on his various activities. Following one such incident the already ailing Prince Albert came to remonstrate with his son, to die of a fever shortly afterwards. Victoria, deeply grieving, never revisited Cambridge again. Now it was time to grieve for her.

CDN 23.1.1901

DEATH OF
Queen Victoria.

HER MAJESTY SINKS SLOWLY TO RES

SCENE AT THE BEDSIDE.

THE WORLD IN MOURNING.

JANUARY 23 1901

Reception of the News
In Cambridge.

The melancholy news, which everyone knew could not be long delayed, of the death of Queen Victoria was received in Cambridge shortly after seven o'clock on Wednesday evening in this brief announcement—" The Queen passed away at 6.30." A feeling of profound sympathy had prevailed throughout the Royal patient's illness, and when at length the death announcement arrived there was universal sorrow and gloom. The *Cambridge Daily News* first gave publicity to the melancholy event to those who in Cambridge were waiting with anxiety for the latest intelligence, and almost simultaneously telegrams were posted at the University Union Society in Trinity - street and at the Guildhall. Shortly afterwards, too, the brief message conveyed to the Lord Mayor at the Mansion House by the Prince of Wales was transmitted to Cambridge, and naturally served to deepen the gloom that already prevailed. The tolling of bells at many of the churches and college chapels also served to spread the sad news, and this (Wednesday) morning the borough bore a complete aspect of mourning for the loss of our beloved Queen. At the churches, the colleges, the Guildhall, and other public institutions, the political clubs, the local banks, and many private residences, Royal Standards are flying half-mast, black ties and other emblems of mourning are being worn by members of the University and the townsmen. Blinds are drawn in numberless cases, and black shutters appear at the windows of almost all business establishments in the borough. As soon as the painful intelligence was received it was conveyed to the New Theatre, where a large number of people had already assembled in anticipation of the night's performance. The news was received by the audience in silence, and then the announcement was made that the performance would not take place. Those who had assembled therefore had their money returned and the building. Nearly all gatherings of a public or social character have been postponed, including the chamber concert which was to have taken place this (Wednesday) evening at the Guildhall.

The proclamation of King Edward VII in the Senate House on 25 January 1901 was repeated outside by the University Registrary in front of a massive crowd, amongst which can be seen a photographer, his bulky camera standing high above the heads of the onlookers. The ceremony was repeated next day by the High Sheriff on behalf of the county at Shire Hall and Hyde Park Corner and by the Mayor in five places, from Market Hill to Mill Road and Newmarket Road. The proclamations took place on different days owing to administrative confusion. It had, of course, been many years since such a ceremony had been performed.   *S.1901 196*

The Coronation originally scheduled for June 1902 had to be postponed owing to the new King's illness. One part of the festivities was a display of decorated floats including this from the Wanderers Cycle Club featuring some of the cups held by their members.

S.1902 29557

In many ways the Cambridge of that time would seem largely familiar both to the Victorians and to us today. St John's Street with undergraduates in cap and gown enjoying the spring sunshine. The Divinity School and the chapel of St John's College – both about 40 years old – can be seen in the background.

B.Joh.K0 39024

King's Parade with St Mary the Great Church and the buildings of Gonville and Caius college on the left, then only 40 years old.
B.Kin.K0 42387

Trumpington Street with the Fitzwilliam Museum. A lady with pram is negotiating a bridge across the channels which run down either side of the street, designed to bring a supply of running water into the town. A new piped water supply from wells at Fulbourn was started in 1891, but in 1907 they were found to be contaminated by sewage from the Asylum. *B.Tru.K0 38986*

Important changes had recently occurred in the relationship between university and town authorities. The university had given up its rights to arrest women found 'walking' with undergraduates. The 'Spinning House', its forbidding private prison in St Andrew's Street, was demolished. *B.And.K0 15585*

The 'Spinning House' was replaced by a new police and fire station, opened 1901, while about the same time the adjacent Baptist Chapel was also rebuilt to provide a new look to St Andrew's Street. On the right stands the New Theatre, opened 1896, in anticipation of the university relaxing its powers to ban plays during term time.   *B.And.K0 39102*

Changes were taking place elsewhere as the university continued its development into scientific research with the opening, by the new King in 1904, of the Downing Street laboratories (left) standing opposite the New Museums which had been initiated by Prince Albert's reforms.   *B.Dow.K0 39107*

The opening was followed by one of the largest of the series of undergraduate riots, known as 'Rags', and the Metropolitan Police had to be drafted in to control the crowds. In 1901 serious rioting had taken place on Market Hill when new underground toilets were ransacked for material to fuel a bonfire and police attempts to control the situation fought off. Such scenes were captured by Harry Moden, one of two cartoonists of the time. These excesses were regarded tolerantly – the young gentlemen being allowed a bit of high spirits.
V.W.K05 4206

Serious incidents of undergraduate misbehaviour – offending university rather than town sensibilities – could result in the student being 'sent down'. The offender was seen off by his colleagues *en route* to the station in an elaborate mock funeral. In 1911 this comprised a parade of some 100 horse and motor vehicles with a brass band on a coal wagon leading the way. Here another group make the journey along Hills Road, passing Cambridge Place, in 1913.
V.WF.K13 47420

One of the town's great celebrations was the Mammoth Show, held on Jesus Green on August Bank Holiday, which included a competition for decorated carriages, here seen on parade turning from Burleigh Street into Fitzroy Street with Eden Baptist chapel on the corner.   *B.Bur.K1 44834*

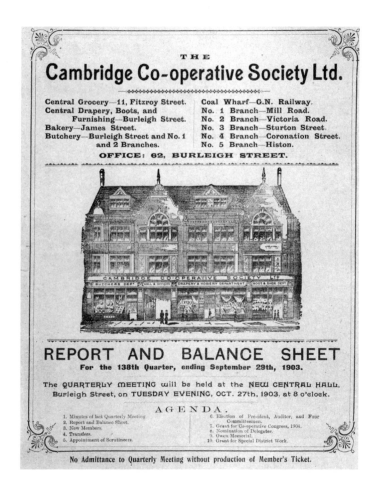

The Co-operative Society opened a new large shop in Burleigh Street in 1900.

P.Co-op.K03 40352

This was an area of small shops serving the local community – such as Laurie Haynes' post office and grocer's shop in Norfolk Street with its variety of commodities and long opening hours.
P.Hayn.K1 47421

At about the same time Laurie & McConnal built a large store in Fitzroy Street which was destroyed by fire in 1903. Items salvaged from the rubble were sold off and a new shop arose from the ashes.   *P.Laur.K03 40907*

The new Laurie & McConnal shop was topped by a bandstand – from which concerts were given – glimpsed in the background to this view of New Square with its rough meadow on which cattle graze as elegant ladies and gentlemen stroll towards Christ's Pieces and the historic town centre.   *B.New.K0 38979*

Elegance, too, along Mill Road which had grown up in the open fields following the Enclosure Acts of 1806-07, part of the massive development of the early Victorian period and was now a thriving housing and commercial centre. *B.Mill.K0 30889*

Even the Workhouse, opened 1838, could look attractive. By 1906 it was known as the Poor Law Infirmary offering rehabilitation, night accommodation for itinerants and care for homeless and single mothers. *I.EA.K0 44642*

Across the railway bridge was Romsey Town, where in 1905 crowds gathered to mark the funeral of Annie Thompson, one of three people drowned in a tragedy at Fen Ditton when an overcrowded ferry sank during the May Week races.   *B.Mill.K05 6941*

Bumping races – so called as the river is too narrow to allow rowing side by side so lines of boats chase and bump the one ahead – were great social occasions with elegant crowds lining the river banks to watch, some in 1910 taking advantage of the recently arrived punts.   *U.ROW.K10 879*

The ferries provided the main river crossing between Cambridge and its northern neighbour, Chesterton, until they were replaced by footbridges in the 1920s. The ferries, although picturesque, were inconvenient, causing delays to people who wished to cross. When ferrymen were not on duty passengers might need to pull the ferry to their side of the river using the damp and weedy chain that ran across the river before winding their way to the other bank. *K.F.K0 39055*

Chesterton residents were near enough to enjoy the facilities of Cambridge but did not have to pay the Cambridge rates and remained independent until 1912 although Cambridge had built the Victoria Bridge in 1890 as one way of encouraging the amalgamation of the two areas. *K.BC.K0 39059*

Victoria Avenue was an impressive road across Midsummer Common, built for horse-drawn traffic. It links Maids Causeway and Jesus Lane to Chesterton Road.

B.Vict.K039088

Chesterton Road, where in 1909 – shortly after this picture was taken – Mr Mitcham opened a shop which gave its name to the junction, seen here centre right. The shop closed in 1977.

B.Ches.K0 20825

Beyond on the right, new lines of elegant houses were growing up in the leafy streets around De Freville Avenue. *B.Frev.K0 39096*

Then came the old village of Chesterton where the Wheatsheaf pub stood opposite the Bleeding Heart in the High Street, all of which have been replaced. *B.Chest.K07 18122*

To the north of Mitcham's Corner were the open spaces of Milton Road with its view across to the windmill in what was to become Hurst Park Avenue. Cambridge Town Football Club later built its ground on the allotment land on the left, opening in 1922. *IX.1*

To the west, down Victoria Road, was New Chesterton, another area of Victorian development, dominated by St Luke's Church, built in 1874. *B.Vic.K0 39132*

St Luke's Church is glimpsed again from the corner of Carlyle Road. *B.Carl.K0 39103*

A new pleasure garden, the Alexandra Gardens, was built on the site of old brickpits and opened in 1907. *J.Ale.K0 40349*

Chesterton Lane led to the crossroads at the bottom of Castle Hill, described as 'a gathering place for the workshy' in 1908 when Northampton Street was widened to cope with traffic. The buildings on the left leading to the junction with Magdalene Street were demolished by the college in 1912.   *B.Che.K0 39119*

Turning right up Castle Hill led into one of the oldest and poorest areas of the town. The Three Tuns (seen here in 1903 and demolished in 1936) is one of the many places where Dick Turpin is said to have stayed.   *V*

The Three Tuns stood just across the road from the County Gaol and Assize Courts which were used by the County Council as a Council Chamber, although its offices were scattered throughout the town until a new County Hall was opened in Hobson Street in 1914. *B.Cas.K0 39119*

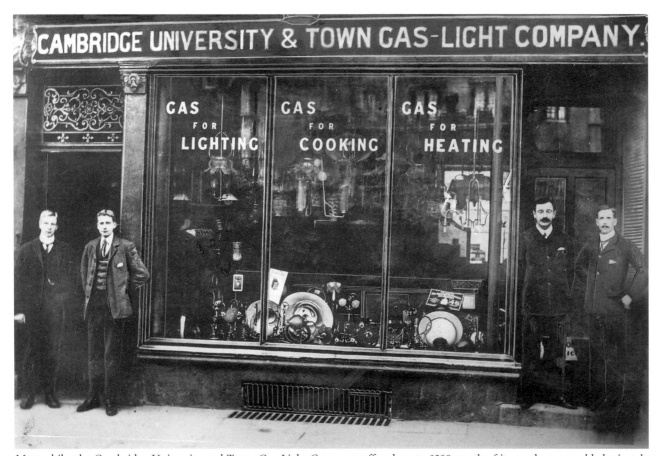

Meanwhile, the Cambridge University and Town Gas-Light Company offered up to £300 worth of its products, payable by instalments, in 1904. *P.Gas.K08 33663*

One urgent issue was the clearing of slums in the Castle Hill area. This had the effect of ousting poor families from their homes but they could not afford the replacement houses and either moved in with neighbours – thus adding to the overcrowding – or went to the workhouse on Mill Road. Here families in Castle Street inspect the damage caused during a lightning strike in June 1908.

B.Cas.K08 11526a

There were complaints in 1910 that whole streets of new houses were being built without a bathroom between them. However, there was now the option of the luxury of electric lighting, powered from a generating station in Thompson's Lane built in 1892.

P.Ele.K09 14326

SUPPOSED SUFFRAGETTE INCENDIARISM.

FIRES AT STOREY'S WAY, CAMBRIDGE.

Photo.]   [Scott & Wilkinson.

House in Storey's Way, Cambridge, just completed for Mrs. Spencer, of 100, Castle-street, which was destroyed by fire in the early hours of Saturday morning last. A young school teacher, a suffragette, has been arrested and charged with causing the fire. She was traced by a gold watch found in an adjoining house, which was also fired.

One luxury house in Storey's Way was destroyed by arson by a suffragette in 1913, her gold watch found in the ruins leading to her arrest, subsequent conviction and hunger strike.

RA.Suf.K13 26515

It was part of the fight for votes for women, which saw colleges closing their gates during the Long Vacation in fear of outrages. This National Union of Suffrage march in 1913 is blocking traffic in St John's Street.   *RA.Suf.K13 36515*

However, public transport was on the move. Horse buses were on their last legs, ceasing in 1902. They had competed with horse trams which had started in 1880 and operated between the Railway Station and Market Hill – seen here – with another branch along East Road to the tram shed.   *Q.Ae.K1 34624*

But trams were challenged by the arrival of the motor bus. An initial experiment with two rival companies in 1905 lasted for only two years but then a new company called 'Ortona' came on the scene in 1907. Although limited to 12 mph they were quicker than the trams which finally expired in 1914.   *Q.Af.K1 33009*

There were now new forms of personal transport – motor cars and motorbikes. An undergraduate, the Hon C.S. Rolls, had been the first man to have a car in Cambridge in 1897, and in 1898 he had ridden a motorcycle inside the Corn Exchange, the venue for this motor show.   *I.O.K1 42778*

Others were displayed in the street, as here in 1910 during a rally by the Cambridgeshire Motor and Cycle Club in Mount Pleasant.

Q.Am.K10 38494

Then, of course, Mount Pleasant was an area more used to other horse power.   *B.Mou.K0 38992*

By 1905 there were claims that no town in England had a greater traffic problem than Cambridge in term time. One car is glimpsed here outside Foster's Bank in Sidney Street (motoring was always an expensive operation). *B.And.K0 39116*

Motor cars are not in evidence in this view of St Andrew's Street, decorated for the Coronation of King George V in 1911. Post Office Terrace is on the right, with Robert Sayle's and the Belfast Linen Company amongst the shops and St Andrew's Street Baptist Church in the background. *B.And.K11 25633*

The bustle of Petty Curry where there seems no room for cars.   *B.Pet.KO 30901*

King George V's reign was not to prove a peaceful one – and not just in Cambridge where[above] the grads in their gowns outside the grandeur of the Senate House contrast with children on parade in Castle Street. In 1908 the newspaper captioned this picture [below] 'Their country's future defenders' – a prophetic statement indeed.

V.U.K1 42754 &T.R.K08 32739

The children were old enough to march alongside troops on Stourbridge Common in 1912, during large-scale army manoeuvres.

T.G.K12 36513

And two years later it was for real when troops assembled on Cambridge commons – here Jesus Green – before marching off to war

T.G.K14 21577

Sir John French inspecting members of the Officer Cadet Corps and Territorial recruits on Parker's Piece, June 1916.

T.G.K16 42760

As local men enlisted, so women took their places in various jobs and industries, here street sweeping in 1917. *PC.Dus.K17 16689*

As the number of undergraduates decreased, the colleges instead opened their doors and facilities to the training of officers, with mock tank battles on the Gogs and grenade practice on Parker's Piece.   *T.G.K14 31748*

Soon the casualties of war were arriving back at Cambridge where a large Military Hospital was established at the Backs of the colleges off Burrell's Walk.   *RM.42*

Left: The war involved troops from around the world, bringing Americans – and their sport – to Cambridge in 1918.

S.1918 43118

Below: There were spontaneous celebrations on Market Hill at the Armistice in November 1918.

S.1918 12742

A Peace Day Festival was held in July 1919 with uniformed and demobilised soldiers turning from Petty Cury into St Andrew's Street *en route* to a huge dinner on Parker's Piece.   *S.1919 13506*

The 1920s

July 1922 saw the unveiling of a memorial to 'Victory' by the Duke of York (the future King George VI). Unfortunately the actual bronze statue was not finished and a plaster cast painted bronze had to be substituted, causing organisers to fear the rain which fell in torrents would make the colouring run. Thousands turned out to watch the ceremony.   *L.War.K22 2603*

The first Poppy Day collection was made in 1921 but undergraduate requests to be allowed to participate were originally resisted, Armistice Day (11 November) being considered too near the Guy Fawkes celebrations of six days earlier when rowdiness was at its height. They were given the opportunity in 1922 when a procession of 'animals' toured the town with a police escort. The experiment was considered a success and became part of the annual scene.   *V.WP.K2 41401*

Dale's Brewery supplied a lorry for this 1928 procession, while Miller's Music Shop used this photograph to advertise 'Every kind of musical instrument supplied to Dance Bands for all occasions'. *V.WP.K28 38918*

Students attracted less support for their activities during the General Strike of 1926 when they helped keep the railways moving while the town railway workers joined the protest. *S.1926 13174*

The Labour Party was making political strides with the foundation stone of the Romsey Labour Club laid by Ramsey McDonald in 1926, although they had to wait until 1937 before the first Labour Mayor, Bill Briggs, was elected. This cartoon was one of many drawn by Ronald Searle during his period with the *Cambridge Daily News* immediately before World War Two. *RA.Lab.K37 47422*

On the labour front traditional jobs – like corn merchants in the Corn Exchange (which continued to trade until 1965) were being joined by new trades. *I.O.K2 33527*

Pye started manufacturing wireless sets in 1921 when there was a lapse in demand for its instruments. "Cambridge is a splendid site for industry" the Chamber of Commerce claimed in 1922, sparking a controversy that would echo for decades.   *P.Pye.K2 8484*

Youngsters found work as delivery boys – here at corner of Honey Hill and Northampton Street – but were replaced as soon as they got older.
B.Nor.K2 16165

Traditional methods of transport – delivery boys on their bicycles and milkroundsmen with their horses and carts (above), this one from Manor Farm Dairy in the open fields off Arbury Road – were being joined by new – a postman (below) with a motor van in Owlstone Road, Newnham where considerable building activity had resulted in a trebling of the pre-war population.

PC.Mil.K2 33492 & B.Owl.K25 3929

A new industry was already established to cope with the new demand for cars; Marshalls had founded its first garage in 1909 and moved to King Street and Jesus Lane in 1912, while the Cambridge Service Motor Company, 'automobile engineers' set up in Hobson Street on the site of what was to become the Central Cinema in 1921.   *IX*

Great FORD Display Week.

MARCH 31st to APRIL 6th.

N'T MISS
SEEING
E ALL
BRITISH
URING
CAR.

Special
Demonstratio
of
Commercial
CARS,
VANS,
LORRIES.

ALL MODELS ON VIEW IN OUR SHOWROOMS.

CAMBRIDGESHIRE MOTORS, LTD.,

Ford Service Depot,

HILLS ROAD, CAMBRIDGE.

10 Demountable Rims, £5 extra.   Tel: 938.   **AUTHORISED DEALERS.**   Grams: FORDS.
   Self Starter, £15 extra

£145   At Works, Manchester.

Cambridgeshire Motors built a new garage on an open-field site at the corner of Cherry Hinton Road – seen here in an advertisement of March 1924 – its distance from the town centre no deterrent to trade.   *P.Cam.K24 2534*

Extra cars needed more parking spaces – in 1926 a motorist was told it was irresponsible to leave his car parked for 25 minutes. The proposal to take a strip of Christ's Pieces for a new car and bus park at Drummer Street met stiff opposition, but it opened in 1925
.
B.Dru.K2 7647

By 1927, Drummer Street car-park was considered too small and agitation started for another on the grassed area of New Square, this time there was less resistance and it opened in 1932.
B.New.K32 16264

One-way systems started in Market Street and Petty Cury in 1925 and the university took steps to restrict the use of cars by students, but problems continued as here at the junction of Emmanuel Street and St Andrew's Street, November *1929.*

Q.Al.K29 47423

One answer was the introduction of traffic lights at the junction of Castle Street and Northampton Street in 1927 to replace the policeman on point duty (although some reported that additional police were required to keep back onlookers and cope with the accidents that occurred).

B.Nor K3 31580

Proposals for a new road across Coe Fen to relieve Silver Street and make better communication between the expanding Newnham area and the town had been aired in 1904 and revived in 1922. They were greeted with sustained protests by those who considered the road would be ugly and spoil the tranquillity of Coe Fen and Sheep's Green.   *J.She.K3 32051*

I shuddered to think of the changing fen.

God ! What shall we do with these wicked men ?

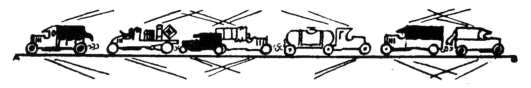

But Fen Causeway opened in 1926, built as part of a labour creation scheme during the time of depression. Ninety unemployed men had been found work on the scheme. *Nelson*

In a period of severe unemployment, jobs in the Cambridge building industry were secured with a major council house building programme. One development was the Rock Estate, off Cherry Hinton Road, while the completion of Hills Avenue was anticipated with great excitement in March 1921.

B.Cher.K22 5491 & B.Hill K21 3584

Building continued in Chesterton, where the landscape was transformed as here at Scotland Road-Green End Road junction between 1927 & 1930.   *B.Sco.K2 11324 & B.Sco.K30 3957*

FROM SLUMS TO SUNSHINE.

Here are the first twenty-two houses to be built under the auspices of the Cambridge Housing Society, Ltd., whose object is to provide decent houses for large families living in Cambridge under crowded and insanitary conditions, who cannot afford the rent of a Council house. These houses stand in Green End Road, and the only "complaint" so far received from the tenants is that "it is so healthy the children eat so much." The

Not all could afford the council rents and the Cambridge Housing Society was established to provide homes for large families, as here at Green End Road, November 1927. *B.Gre.K27 2689*

For the more affluent, council houses on Coldhams Lane and Milton Road – seen here from junction of Arbury Road – were offered for sale in 1927 at a price of £579, payable in weekly instalments of 21s 1d (£1.05). *B.Milt.K2 36344*

Above and below: There was more building along Histon Road in 1932, soon linked by a new Gilbert Road, its first houses facing across open countryside towards Arbury Road [below].   *B.His.K32 3143 &*
B.Gil.K33 14693

New forms of prefabricated construction were tried in King's Hedges Road in 1927. Here giant cranes are lifting panels into place.
B.Milt.K27 36346

Innovative architectural styles were also built in more central areas, as here at Pinehurst flats off Grange Road, 1933.

B.Gran.K3 15340

Development spread between Cherry Hinton Road and Mill Road creating new streets such as Coleridge Road in 1924 and Perne Road in 1933 (seen here in 1937).

B.Pern.K37 37178

The developments also brought new facilities, such as these shops in Vinery Road (seen in 1945).   *B.Vine.K45 24077*

New schools also opened. These children are picking wild flowers outside Sedley School, Malta Road, which opened in 1932. It was the first with up-to-date nurseries for infants and broke tradition with single-storey classrooms around an open grassed courtyard
.
                                                                                            G.Sed.K3 47423

Additional entertainment facilities included new cinemas such as the Tivoli in Chesterton Road which became the second purpose-built cinema when it opened in 1925.   *B.Ches.K25 4264*

An innovative new theatre – The Festival – opened in 1926, making Newmarket Road the cultural centre of Cambridge. Here we are looking towards the town with the junction with East Road on the left, 1928.   *B.Newm.K28 16347*

In the countryside, just beyond the Leper Chapel, Marshall opened an airfield with a flying display which brought aviation enthusiasts from around the country, including Sir Alan Cobban whose aircraft can be seen to the right of the figure in plus-fours – Arthur (later Sir Arthur) Marshall, 1938.   *P.Mars.K38 33133*

The area's other landmarks were the brickworks which stretched from Coldham's Lane alongside the railway line, producing the white bricks which fuelled the building boom.   *P.Swa.K24 13286*

On the other side of the road the gas works were expanded with a new coke handling plant in 1923, the biggest gas-holder in East Anglia in 1927 and the rebuilding of its Coldham's Lane railway sidings in 1929. This led to additional heavy motor traffic and the final demise of river trade to Cambridge when the barges that collected ammonia water from the works ceased in 1933.

P.Gas.K27 13019

Now punts predominated where once ocean-going craft had moored at Mill Pool, and a new vista opened on the properties clustered along Granta Place, including the Belle Vue Hotel which had opened in the Garden House in 1923. *VIII*

Another connection with the trading past was removed with the demolition of the ancient King's and Bishop's Watermills on Mill Pool in 1927. These had been established long before the university and had marked the head of navigation for the barges which had plied along the Backs until the coming of the railways in 1845.   *V111.2*

Meanwhile in the town centre the view of King's College was enhanced with the removal in 1927 of the heavy railings which had formerly stretched right along to the Senate House. A low wall was to be built in 1932. *B.Kin.K2 36368*

The 1930s

THIRD DEATH IN SHOOTING DRAMA

TRIPLE TRAGEDY OF KING'S

Detective Willis Dies from Wounds

INQUEST ON FRIDAY

Undergraduate's Debts to Local Tradesmen

The third of the principals in the King's College shooting sensation yesterday afternoon, Det.-Sergt Willis, died in Addenbrooke's Hospital this morning from the effects of his wounds.

The undergraduate assailant, Douglas Newton Potts, died in Addenbrooke's Hospital shortly before six p.m. yesterday, from a bullet wound in the head.

Mr. Wollaston, the tutor, was killed instantly, the shot passing through his heart.

Potts, it is now stated, went away from Cambridge nine days ago with another undergraduate, Mr. Newman, of Fitzwilliam House, on a motor-cycle obtained on credit.

A sensational story by a London woman as to their staying with her in Town appears in column 5.

The police wished to interview Potts in connection with certain complaints, and it was this, combined with Potts' excitable temperament, that led to the tragedy.

THE SHOOTING

Detective's Attempt to Save Tutor

HEAVILY IN DEBT

Why the Police Wanted to See Potts

The Late Detective Sergeant Willis

A POPULAR OFFICER

Served Throughout the War Without a Wound

THE LATE MR. A. F. R. WOLLASTON

Royal Geographical Society's Tribute

POTTS IN LONDON

Woman's Remarkable Story

'CLEANING PISTOLS'

A KNOCK AT THE DOOR

IN TROUBLE AT CAMBRIDGE

'WOULD END THINGS'

CARTRIDGES ON TABLE

AT THE "43" AND MANHATTAN CLUBS

CONDUCTOR OF JAZZ BAND

SUICIDE'S FAILING SIGHT

Cambridge Woman's Worries

HUSBAND'S TRAGIC DISCOVERY

Above: In June 1930, murder rocked King's College when an undergraduate shot his tutor and a Cambridge policeman, Detective-Sergeant Willis, before killing himself. *Below:* Coincidentally 1930 was the same year that the Cambridge gallows were sold off – they had been last used to hang a murderer in 1913 – but few takers were found.
I.G. K30 44182

The gallows formed part of the old County Gaol at Castle Hill which had closed in 1916. Some 8,000 people took the opportunity for a tour of inspection in June 1930 before the buildings were demolished. *I.G.K30 42761*

Some of the bricks from the County Gaol were reused in the county council's new Shire Hall which opened on the site in 1932. This prompted the town council to reconsider its own Guildhall accommodation and they debated moving from Market Hill to a site on Parkside, away from the traffic problems of the town centre. *B.Pa.K3 45360*

Cambridge won one battle with the county when its application for additional land was granted by the Government in 1934 and borough boundaries were extended to take in areas of rural Cherry Hinton where residents were already fearing urbanisation. Both pictures show Church End, where the church and school were separated from the rest of the High Street by the railway crossing.

Y.Cher K2 24726 &
Y.Cher.K2 24723

The expanded boundaries also embraced Trumpington, where the 'Tally Ho' pub now catered for cars rather than coaches and lines of houses stretched along the road to Shelford.

Y.Tru.K3 24215 &
Y.Tru.K3 24318

Such ribbon development prompted the Cambridge
Preservation Society in 1937 to launch a campaign to
restrict building towards the Gogs.   *Brochure*

The University Library was opened by King George V
and Queen Mary in 1934.   *F.B.K34 47424*

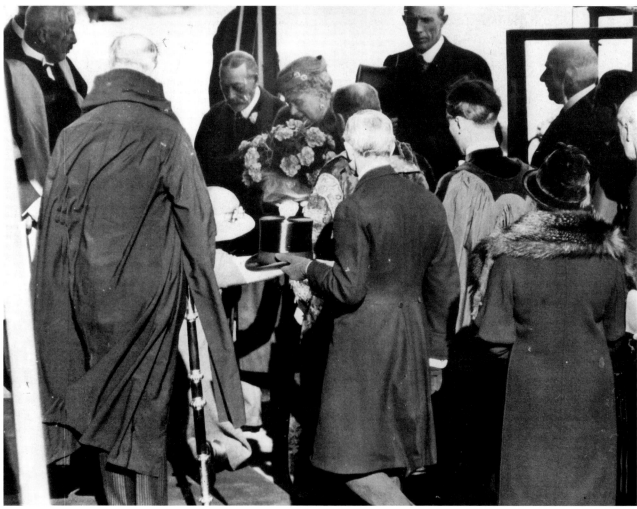

Meanwhile the building boom that continued in the suburbs was being echoed in the town centre. When the old military hospital huts came down, Clare College built a Memorial Court and a new University Library arose on the site.

F.B. K34 35659

Magdalene College building plans for student accommodation resulted in the demolition of Fisher Lane, see here from Magdalene Bridge looking towards St John's College.   *III.35*

However, proposals to rebuild the whole of the west side of Magdalene Street were shelved when the college hit financial difficulties, the architect's plans envisaging a much wider street.   *B.Mag.K28 11685*

Above: Nearer town, however, these shops on the west side of Bridge Street were removed for a new Music School for St John's College.   *1X*

Right: The building work for the Music School is seen in this 1937 view from the college chapel tower which also looks across to the Union Society building behind the Round Church.

A.1937 11701

In Hobson Street, the Central Cinema was rebuilt in 1930, contrasting with the old garage it replaced.   *I.L.K3 20126*

Above and opposite page: Further along the junction with Sussex Street was redeveloped to match.

B.Sus.K2 6943
& B.Hob.K35 26099

The process was repeated in Sidney Street with a new Dorothy Café/Restaurant and Dance Hall offering a whole new entertainment facility.

B.Sid.K29 2336

Rebuilding continued along the east side of the street, bringing new shops – Heffers, Sainsbury, Woolworth – and wider footpaths – a cutting of 17 October 1936. *B.Sid.K36 30802*

The scheme was matched on the other side of the street with a massive new Boots store extending from Sidney Street into Petty Cury
B.Sid.K3 45359

From some angles Petty Cury seemed largely unaltered as from Market Hill with Heffers Bookshop, the Lion Hotel and the decorations for the Coronation of King George VI in 1937.   *IX.1*

'Never has Cambridge witnessed so much pulling down and building up,' the newspaper commented in 1935 when the west side of Peas Hill between St Edward's Church & Bene't Street was rebuilt leading to the opening of the Arts Theatre in 1936.

B.Pea.K3 47425

The traditional fish market in Peas Hill – with the Bell public house on the right and the Central Hotel in the middle distance – was forced off the street because of increasing traffic.
B.Pea.K30 4239

There was, however, parking for shoppers at the back of the Lion Hotel in Petty Cury.
V.35

In St Andrew's Street one of the most famous inns, The Old Castle Hotel, was destroyed by fire in 1934. *O.Cas.K2 22963*

On the site of The Old Castle Hotel, a new cinema, the Regal, opened in April 1937. *I.L.K37 6639*

The Regal stood just opposite the New Theatre which was itself showing films as it competed with the new Arts Theatre, although the Festival was by now also experiencing difficulties and soon closed. *I.L.K3 20135*

Another new cinema had opened on Market Hill in 1931 – the Victoria, having been established as the Electric Cinema in 1912, in what became the Eastern Electricity showroom. Flags celebrate the Coronation of 1937.   *ix.3*

This was just part of a massive rebuilding of the Square. On the north side Bacon's, Cambridge's leading tobacconist who had traded on the site since about 1820, moved temporarily to the other side of Rose Crescent.   *B.Mar.K34 7393*

Meanwhile, a new development of student rooms for Gonville and Caius College was constructed – here partially finished – in the background to the civic celebrations of the Silver Jubilee of King George V in 1935. *S.1935 45337*

The Borough Council had finally agreed to rebuild the Guildhall on its old site, starting with the demolition of houses and shops on the corner of Peas Hill and Market Hill. Scaffolding from other building work is visible in the background. *B.Pea.K3 47426*

The first stage of the new Guildhall was constructed along the side of Peas Hill. The monumental architecture dominated the old building alongside, which was then removed and rebuilt to join up. The light line in the brickwork under the central windows of the old Guildhall (below) shows where the the canopy which formerly shielded the entrance had to be demolished when it became dangerous in 1933.   *I.A.K35 109*

One council decision had been to push for the closure of the centuries-old Stourbridge Fair, once the greatest in Europe. It was finally abolished in 1935, although Midsummer Fair continued, its crockery stalls and amusements attracting crowds, as did its hot-pea stalls.   *V.H.K3 45540*

At Easter there were also stalls in Parkside selling novelties such as tinsel-covered balls on elastic.   *VII.28*

The stalls on Parkside supplemented the traditional Good Friday celebrations on Parker's Piece, said to mark the publicans' day out when they came for a game of bat and trap, while youngsters amused themselves skipping with ropes normally used to secure the barrels on the brewers' wagons.   *V11.27*

Others queued to watch other sights – the Coronation of King George VI in 1937 providing the occasion for the first public showing of television in Cambridge, in a tent in Sedley Taylor Road.   *W.27.85.K37 41356*

Once more the streets were decorated as here in Regent Street. On the right is the glass porch of the University Arms Hotel where Oswald Mosley addressed meetings of fascists in 1933 and 1935.   *IX.1*

Undergraduates demonstrated against fascism, supported the ideals of communism, enlisted with the International Brigade in the Spanish Civil War and celebrated the Spirit of Munich with impersonations of Chamberlain and Hitler during the Rag in 1938.

V.WP.K38 44622

Of course, undergraduates also indulged in more traditional
Poppy Day frivolities, as here in St Andrew's Street in 1937.
                                                V.WP.K37 17837

Alas, the May Balls in June 1939 – as here at King's – were destined to be the last in peacetime as the long-expected war arrived.
                                                                                        V.Q.K39 44798

Cambridge at War

With the declaration of war King's College authorities decided to remove the medieval stained glass from the windows of the chapel – although some asked what was the point of saving glass if the chapel itself was destroyed. *S.1939 44285*

Throughout the town precautions were taken, windows taped to prevent them fragmenting in the event of bomb blast and public buildings sandbagged, as here at the old Post Office buildings on the corner of Petty Cury. Air-raid shelters were constructed, including those at the strongrooms of Lloyd's Bank.
S.1939 44282

Air Raid precautions were practised – here men are dealing with a supposed gas-attack on Mill Road storeyard – and first-aid posts established, including one for pets in Lion Yard.
S.1938 37183

While Cambridge prepared for bombing, others fled to the town for safety. Child evacuees from London were to be joined by war-workers from firms which were relocated and Civil Servants based at offices in Brooklands Avenue. As undergraduate numbers declined, colleges became home to students from London University and to military training units. *S.1939 20144*

Home Guard forces were mobilised, prepared to defend the town to the last bomb, last bullet and last man. Here the 5th Battalion are practising cliff scaling with their guns at Cherry Hinton chalk pit in 1943. *T.G.K43 42964*

Marshall's airfield, which had opened on its present site in 1938 with a display of Spitfires, became actively involved in the war effort, maintaining and repairing damaged aircraft and undertaking conversion work on the Mosquito, making it the principal home defence night fighter from 1943 to 1944.
Q.C.K38 33162

Ten people were killed at Vicarage Terrace during the first bombing raid in June 1940 and, although never blitzed, Cambridge was bombed on various occasions. The headline in the newspaper report of 31 January 1941 refers to the housewife calmly brushing dust from her windows when the house next door in Mill Road was shattered, but it might equally summarise the war effort in Cambridge where university work and research continued despite everything.
S.1941 26845

From 1943, Cambridge became a centre of rest and recuperation for American troops and airmen from the numerous bases which were established in the vicinity. Some unkind folk claimed that more damage was caused by the troops based in the town than by German air raids.
S.1944 45037

Plans for the D-Day landings were rehearsed when Generals Eisenhower and Montgomery came to Cambridge in March 1944 and the American Cemetery at Madingley was dedicated on the day invasion was due to have taken place.   *M.Ame.K4 40448*

The success of the operation led ultimately to Victory in Europe, celebrated by crowds on Market Hill   *S.1945 43644*

Victory over fascism saw street parties throughout the town – as seen here in Gwydir Street, partly blocked by the air-raid shelter.

B.Gwy.K45 24021

Celebrations, though, were not complete until the men of the Cambridgeshire Regiment, who had been captured following the fall of Singapore, finally came home and paraded with their flags and drums to receive the Freedom of the Borough in 1946.

T.G.K46 32776

Into the 1950s

With the return of peace the number of undergraduates rose. In 1946 some 90 per cent of the places were filled by ex-servicemen, bringing a new maturity, although in 1948 a hand-grenade was thrown at the Senate House as somebody's idea of Guy Fawkes Night celebration. Usually, though, rag stunts continued to amuse both Town and Gown – and police tolerated them.   *V.WP.K5 27916*

University life was changing significantly. During the war, students from Woolwich and Sandhurst had been admitted to Cambridge without the previous requirements of a knowledge of Latin and Greek. The changing place of women within the university was acknowledged when the Queen became the first woman to be admitted to full membership of the university, receiving an Honorary degree in October 1948. The women's colleges of Girton and Newnham were formally recognised and girls allowed to wear academic dress.

V.U.K46 37093

CAMBRIDGE POPPY DAY REVELS

(1) A dry day for Poppy Day, but a wet one if you don't pay up to the hose operator.   (2) A mobile Chinese Laundry.

Other revels are pictured in the *Cambridge Daily News* of November 1959.

CDN 7.11.59

Both county and town wanted to remove prominent buildings despite protest from the other. The Assize Courts on Castle Hill, with its statues (above) representing Law, Justice, Mercy and Power, were knocked down in April 1953 and the site is now the Shire Hall car-park, while the crumbling top of the Fountain on Market Hill came down the same year – shown below decorated for the Coronation of Queen Elizabeth II.   *CIP 17.4.53 p11 & B.Mar.K53 43971*

The new Queen visited the Guildhall in 1955, four years after King George VI had granted Cambridge the status of City in 1951.

5.12

Queens' College had been threatened with flooding in March 1947 when the Cam burst its banks and the waters of the Mill Pool engulfed Silver Street Bridge.
W.12.K47 16432

Silver Street Bridge was rebuilt in 1958, the skeleton of the new bridge echoing the wooden 'Mathematical Bridge' seen in the background.
K.BB.K58 32412

The new bridge would have to cope with increasing traffic, both under it – as tourism started to grow – and over it as traffic multiplied.
K.P.K58 35671

Coping with traffic – as here at Sidney Street in 1950 – was one of the issues covered in the publication of the County Council's Holford Report intended to chart the way Cambridge should develop in forthcoming years.
B.Sid .K5 36000

New roads were suggested, including one from Petty Cury to St Tibbs Row (shown) – giving access to the Lion Hotel parking area, where more buildings were demolished to make more room.
                                                                                                    B.Tib.K6 44196

In the event no road was built – Petty Cury in the rain.   *B.Pet.K5 42857*

In 1951, the Royal Show was held at Trumpington, its attractions and car-parks sprawling over several acres. It is seen from the north with the old railway line to Bedford curving across the site, the Shelford Road in the background and new houses on Foster Road at the right.   *S.1951 43620*

Nearby other acres were being developed for 'temporary' Unity steel and concrete houses with the 1,000th being opened by Ernest Marples in 1952. That year the Minister also allowed the council to build along Queen Edith's Way, despite county opposition. Here we are looking from Lime Kiln Hill with the chimneys of the Norman Cement Works in the distance.   *A.195 19454*

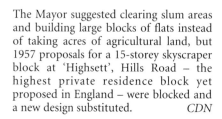

The Mayor suggested clearing slum areas and building large blocks of flats instead of taking acres of agricultural land, but 1957 proposals for a 15-storey skyscraper block at 'Highsett', Hills Road – the highest private residence block yet proposed in England – were blocked and a new design substituted.   *CDN*

Elsewhere a smaller scale complex of old folks' accommodation at Honey Hill off Northampton Street opened in 1956, attracting praise.

B.Hon.K56 40723

By 1953 there was a 15-year waiting list for council homes and plans for a new development off Arbury Road were announced, the estate growing rapidly by 1956.

CDN 16.8.56

Development, too, on the Newmarket Road (centre) with Marshalls in the foreground, The Westering beyond. Houses are being erected in Peverel Road and the outline of Barnwell Road and the Whitehill Estate is etched on the old airfield site in the background.

Q.CA.K48 33202

New facilities followed, such as Netherhall School in 1958 and a branch library in Barnwell Road the same year.   *F.I.K58 4482*

Slum clearance schemes continued. Doric Street and Gothic Street (shown) off Lensfield Road were demolished in 1958.

B.Got.K5 36854

There was more clearance around East Road. Here the junction of Fitzroy Street and Wellington Street as photographed by Percy North.

B.Fit.K6 25704

Percy North then turned his attention to the corner opposite – Nelson Street and the former Duke of Wellington public house. Holford had proposed that a new shopping centre be established in this area.   *B.Fit.K50 3479*

Despite Holford's proposal, the City favoured redevelopment in the centre – the corner of Market Hill and Petty Cury in 1950.

B.Mar.K50 36004

The city, though, did not favour the demolition, for a new college hostel in 1959, of the Central Hotel in Peas Hill, a listed building where Samuel Pepys 'drank pretty hard' in 1660 but latterly a Temperance Hotel. *B.Mar.K5 21356*

There was less opposition to the demolition, in 1957, of Rances Folly – a tall and palatial home of a former Mayor in St Andrew's Street. *B.And.K56 3502*

Other buildings were swept away in 1959 for new shops and offices from the corner of Emmanuel Street (above) leading to the opening of Bradwell's Court – the city's first shopping arcade – seen below in1961.   *Scoon 27681 & 5122*

The Bradwell Court shopping arcade took its name from the old Bradwell's Yard (above) one of many which had offered homes adjacent to central streets demolished during rebuilding, and resulted in the closure of Christ's Lane (below) which had formerly been the main thoroughfare to Drummer Street bus station.

B.Bra.K3 42430 & B.Chr.K5 1556

There was rebuilding, too, on Lensfield Road where the university constructed a new Chemistry Laboratory, dominating the streets of the New Town area, seen in the foreground. Beyond is Downing College, the Downing site and the heart of the university city.
A.1954 41414

Other developments were being scheduled further away from the centre, as anticipated by Holford. Plans for the Sidgwick Avenue Arts Site were announced in 1952 and this new Veterinary School opened in fields off Madingley Road in 1955. *DZ.Vet.K54 41425*

Much fundamental research into nuclear fission and the secret of life itself was being undertaken in the Cavendish laboratories off Free School Lane – chosen as the backdrop for scenes in the film 'Bachelor of Hearts', starring Hardy Kruger and Sylvia Sims, which was filmed in 1958.

E11.0202.26

Meanwhile, as the university were developing computers, Pye researchers were pioneering stereo sound – Christmas celebrations at the factory 1955 – and rock'n'roll arrived.

P.Pye.K5 27406

The 1960s

Rock'n'roll was not welcomed in Cambridge. In 1956 magistrates asked cinemas to ban the film 'Rock Around The Clock' and there were complaints that people were jiving during waltzes at Guildhall dances, despite the ban on such outrageous activity. However, the Rex Ballroom relented in 1957 and Mick Mulligan topped the bill at the Pye Apprentices' Jazz Ball that February.
CDN 16.2.57

Cliff Richard appeared at the Regal in 1959, when vast crowds blocked Regent Street, and soon other pop stars were performing, including Adam Faith, and a few years later the Rolling Stones (pictured).
5470/C

The Beatles, described as 'a four-man rock group' with weird hairstyles as a gimmick, sang and played their current hits, 'Love Me Do' and 'Please Please Me'. 'The fast moving show was not the best Cambridge has seen,' commented the *News* in March 1963. That November, the Beatles returned with a police escort, smuggled in a Black Maria to the Downing Street labs. The queue started at 10.30am and the cinema was like a fortress with the drawbridge up. There were 4,000 in the audience, including these fans from Cambridge who were fortunate enough to meet with their heroes.

Y2618

Not everybody enjoyed it, how-ever. 'Screaming teenagers sparsely mixed with incredulous and slightly-dazed parents . . .the show was deplorably uninteresting but the audience gave a magnificent performance,' said the reviewer of an Adam Faith concert in 1960. *Y2603*

For others joining in was part of the fun. The Folk Festival launched at Cherry Hinton Hall in 1965 soon became an established part of the music scene and was incorporated into the Cambridge Festival.   *3235/D*

Below: Meanwhile, the Madrigals on the river attracted large crowds as in this log-jam of punts in 1961.   *K2308*

The audience for other classical music, however, was limited by the lack of a proper concert hall, the Guildhall providing the only venue for larger orchestras – such as the Chelsea Opera Group seen here – until the opening of the University Music School in West Road in 1977.

5977B

But it was pop music at the fairground, drowning the squeals of the dodgems.   *Scoon 27850*

There were even pop services in Cambridge churches – frost and snow at Great St Mary's in 1967.

Scoon 27555

There was a severe winter in 1963, when the Cam froze and skaters turned out to take the opportunity of enjoying a different view of the Backs. *U.Ska.K5 22413*

In 1964, though, April sunshine brought crowds out at Mill Pool. *Y7005*

Following the May Balls in June 1964, students and their guests prepare to punt down to Grantchester for the traditional breakfast, having danced the night away.   *Y9072*

But partying wasn't confined to the young – a garden party in Downing College Fellows' Garden, September 1962.

Z2544

CAMBRIDGE DAILY NEWS, Friday, May 6, 1960

ids In Student Dress
Beginning Of Another
And Fashion'

Photos : Central Studios, Ramsey

Variations on the current Cambridge sartorial scene caught in the camera. So far as the student male is concerned, at least, clothes are hardly outlandish. For every casual dresser, one may find a formal one.

CYCLIST I

A fine of 25s, w:
James Mayall, of 16
Harpenden, Herts.,
without front and r
wyn Gardens on N
case was heard b;
City Magistrates y

Student dress had changed, now that 80 per cent of the undergraduates were on a grant and boaters and blazers no longer the accepted fashion. In 1960, tailors lamented the trend to jeans and duffel coats, sloppy-joes and 17in trouser bottoms which was to lead to the demise in their trade; "Thirty years ago students were proud of their dress and bought four suits at a time. Now they shuffle around in jeans and sweaters and do not have two halfpennies to rub together," said a spokesman for Pratt, Manning & Co, Cambridge's oldest bespoke tailor, when it closed in 1962.

6.5.60

A fundamental part of undergraduate dress – the gown which had to be worn at lectures and after dark – was abolished in 1965. Walker & Walker, tailors of Market Hill, who had served Edward VII when he was Prince of Wales, closed that year and others followed.

Z3389

The 1960s was a decade of student agitation, protest and demonstrations. Here is pictured a meeting in the Lady Mitchell Hall, part of the new Sidgwick Avenue development.

1641/R

One new student was Prince Charles, who came up to Trinity College in October 1967 – here he is greeted by the Master, Lord Butler – where he was to work for a degree, unlike those Princes who had attended university before him.   *9763/E*

New buildings for the third all-women's college, New Hall, were opened by the Queen Mother in 1965, joining Girton and Newnham as places where men were excluded. Meanwhile, Queens' College scrapped its strict male-female segregation rule, paving the way for a new foundation taking both sexes.   *1477/C*

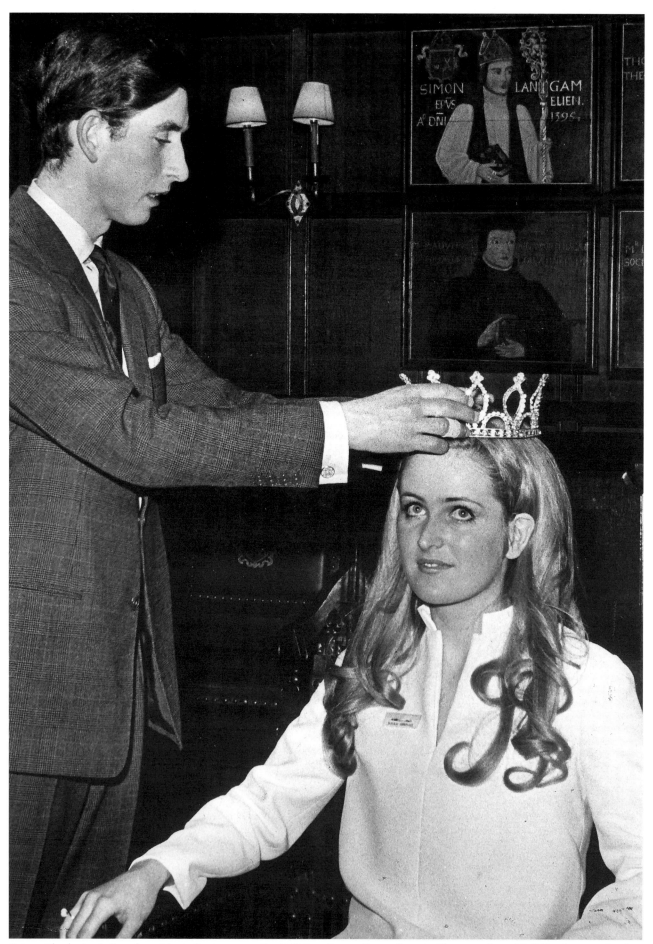

Prince Charles took time from his studies to crown the 1967 Rag Queen, Susan Francis. That year Anne Mallelieu became the first woman president of the Union Society.

10438/P/8

There was a massive programme of new colleges and building, including Darwin (the first graduate college in modern times), Lucy Cavendish (the first graduate college for women), Fitzwilliam, Wolfson and Churchill with its emphasis on science and technology which was opened (above) by the Duke of Edinburgh in 1964. *Y8655*

*There's a **NEW LOOK** too at the famous*

Dorothy RESTAURANT

AND BANQUETING SUITES

The luxurious appointments and decor of the new Blue Room and Venetian Room restaurant suites . . . their quiet and unrivalled elegant atmosphere . . . the superb cuisine . . . all combine to make the 'new' Dorothy the most fashionable restaurant in Cambridge.

The first floor Venetian Room now has full menu services, including Grills, from 9.30 a.m. to 5.30 p.m. daily (Sundays excepted).

✻ Other changes include the enlargement of the characteristic Oak Room, the hitherto Cromwell Room is now known as the Sidney Room, and the large room fronting Hobson Street previously called the New Room now becomes the Sussex Room.

Pictured here is part of the fabulous new Blue Room restaurant on the new Mezzanine floor. With the Venetian Room, Oak Room, Sidney Room, Hobson Room and Sussex Room, it is available for Banquets, Receptions and Parties.

THE CATERING TEAM

The Dorothy owes its popularity to its expert catering team whose wealth of experience is also at your disposal for indoor or outdoor catering of any description. Advice and estimates are free and gladly given — simply telephone 53493.

MR. R. J. CONGDON　MR. M. H. BELLERBY　MR. M. WOLLARD
Catering Manager　　Banqueting Manager　　Chef

✻ **PASSENGER LIFT** to all Floors
✻ **FULLY LICENSED**
✻ **EVENING DANCES** every Wednesday & Saturday

G. P. HAWKINS LTD.　　20/24 SIDNEY STREET • CAMBRIDGE • Tel. 53493

For those not dining on Top Table there were other eating places. The Dorothy Restaurant was revamped in October 1961. It closed in 1977.

Menu

There was also the Civic Restaurant in the old Post Office building in Petty Cury providing good cheap fare – as here in October 1968 – until its closure in 1972. *9447/P/35a*

The Lion Hotel in Petty Cury, seen on the right just beyond Heffers Bookshop, closed in 1963, although its bars remained opened for a while longer. *Y1123*

One of the in-places for the student set was the Turk's Head stable bar in Trinity Street (pictured in 1963, closed 1978), selling sherry from the barrel.   *Y544*

Beer by the barrel was still being produced in the Albion Brewery, Coronation Street, until its closure in 1965. In 1900 there had been 16 breweries in Cambridge. This was down to six by 1925, five by 1950 and the last, the Star Brewery, ceased in 1972.   *Y5320*

Two old-established businesses ceased. Macintosh's ironmongers closed its Market Street shop in 1960, blaming congestion on Market Hill, and Matthew's grocers, Trinity Street, shut its doors for the last time in 1964. After 134 years they were no longer able to offer a traditional grocery service from a large city centre shop at the present rents. Tesco's opened in St Andrew's Street the same year but closed in 1983.

P.Mac.K62 25995

Below: Old established inns also found themselves competing with new arrivals. The Mill, joined by a new University Centre, opened in 1967, its buildings dominating the Mill Pool. *6.25*

A massive new student block, the Cripps Building at St John's, was opened in 1967 just beyond the old Fisher Lane. It is seen here from Magdalene Bridge.   *E.SJ.K71 4256*

Magdalene Bridge was sagging under the weight of traffic. A 12-ton limit had been imposed in 1953, and buses and lorries were banned in 1967, but plans for a replacement met with opposition.   *6053/E*

On the other side of Magdalene Bridge, the Thompson's Lane power station closed in 1966 with work under way to convert 25,000 consumers from its 200 volts to the new standard 250 volts. The work was anticipated to take six years and cost £249,000.

591/D

6053/E

Below: Gas consumers were undergoing similar changes with the introduction of North Sea gas, given priority because of the number of student suicides. Cambridge production ceased in 1969.

A1933 33700

Not all change was welcomed. The rebuilding of King Street to provide student flats for Christ's College – although fine when viewed from the college – was attacked as having destroyed the character of the street.   *B.King.K60 21485*   *& 18928/P19*

These sentiments were also echoed in the New Town area with demolition in Coronation Street, never a particularly attractive section of Cambridge – seen from St Paul's Church tower in 1964. *Y6317*

Demolition in Coronation Street in the 1960's resulted in a mixture of styles, pictured here in 1983.   *6868316*

To the north, building continued with an additional 25 acres between Arbury Road and King's Hedges being sanctioned in 1965. There were inevitably problems – as with flooding at the Edgecombe flats in 1968 – and development on allotments across Histon Road for the McManus Estate and at Church End, Cherry Hinton.   *1026/R*

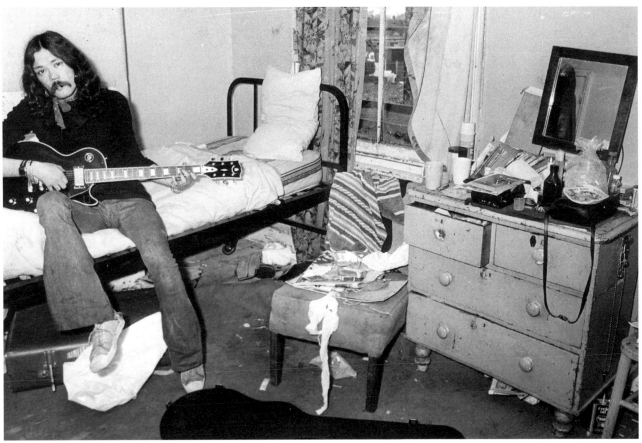

Despite the development of new living accommodation there was still a shortage of 3,000 houses for young couples as well as housing for the less fortunate members of society – and the Salvation Army's White Ribbon Hostel could meet only part of the problem.

40937824

A magnificent indoor swimming pool – described as the finest in the country – opened in April 1963 and new fire and police stations built nearby on Parkside.

Z7351

Other major projects constructed included the first stage of a new Addenbrooke's Hospital. Opened by the Queen in 1962; subsequent stages followed, the second being described as 'an unlovely and inhumane heap' by the *Architects' Journal*. Facilities at the old Addenbrooke's (pictured here in October 1963) were gradually transferred.

H.A.K6 20497 & Y1809.

Above: But planning indecision still affected the Lion Yard and Fitzroy Street proposals and areas crumbled, as here at Occupation Road, off Newmarket Road in 1966. *8686/C*

Left: On the traffic front there were significant developments with Park Street multi-storey opening in October 1963, after plans for an underground car-park on Parker's Piece had been rejected (although they would be reconsidered again and again). *Y.7791*

Parking on Market Hill where cars at night nestled amongst the stalls, as here in 1963, was banned in 1969.   *Y1121*

Then came parking meters in 1964, followed by yellow lines in 1965, as here in Corn Exchange Street, January 1965.   *5110B*

It all did little to ease traffic chaos, as shown by this scene in Downing Street in June 1963.   *Z9266*

Nor were the cycle problems solved, as here in Sidney Street, October 1964. 'Sometimes . . .bikes are parked so closely in line that pedestrians cannot find space to cross over,' the newspaper had commented in 1934.   *2332B*

The problems for ponies speaks for itself – April 1968 in Hills Road.   *25/P/31a*

Mitcham's Corner, where a roundabout had first been installed in 1932 and long a traffic bottleneck both day – here by day in April 1965, and night in January 1966 – was redesigned in 1967.   *165/C & 7645/C*

Traffic congestion at Mitcham's Corner was relieved with the opening of Elizabeth Bridge in 1971 after years of debate – it had been conceived at the same time as Victoria Bridge – and minutes of embarrassment when the golden scissors wielded by Lord Butler failed to cut the ribbon strung across the road.

1420

At first Elizabeth Bridge seemed the answer – 'Like motoring on a Sunday morning,' – but soon 21,000 vehicles a day were using it and numbers increased.   *6.47*

Although reducing traffic on some routes, the approach roads to Elizabeth Bridge had carved through former residential streets, cutting through these houses on Hawthorn Way.   *B.Haw.K6 36657*

Quiet Haig and Cam Roads – seen here in 1965 – became Elizabeth Way.   *B.Cam.K65 32494*

On the other side of the river, Walnut Tree Avenue disappeared altogether for the approach to Newmarket Road.   *Y5110*

The old junction – Walnut Tree Avenue to the left, East Road to the right, seen in 1963 – was transformed by the creation of a new roundabout; Newmarket Road was dualled to feed the junction.   *Z9528 & B.Newm.K70 5718*

Part of East Road was also made dual carriageway. 'The class of traffic makes it one of the most unpleasant thoroughfares in the town,' the newspaper commented in 1914. It is seen here during a relatively calm period in June 1963.   *Z9128*

At the end of East Road a new car-park at Queen Anne Terrace was opened in 1971, although it proved too far from the city centre to attract shoppers.

7568/24

The 1970s

Other road schemes were being debated – a Western Relief Road parallel to Fen Causeway, an Inner Relief Road from Brooklands Avenue to the A45, and, following the longest and most involved enquiry ever seen, a Western bypass (the M11) and a Northern bypass, seen here cutting through Girton during its construction in 1977. It opened in 1978, with the M11 arriving in 1980. No longer did through-traffic need to wend its way into the city. *22907720*

On a foggy morning in February 1975 some city centre roads were closed to cars as pedestrian schemes were introduced, including Sidney Street and Kings Parade – although some people took a while to get used to the idea. *8.2.75*

The most significant road closure was in Petty Cury, where in December 1972 Councillor Chris Gough-Goodman and his friend Jennifer Hall celebrated with lunch in the street.   *3286/37*

The alfresco lunch marked the start of the redevelopment of the Lion Yard area during which the south side of Petty Cury – seen here during a fire in December 1970 – was demolished.   *Z1341*

Also bulldozed was Alexandra Street which linked Petty Cury with Post Office Terrace. This had been built by Corpus Christi College in the 1870s to provide new shops and offices and became home to the National Telephone Company's exchange in 1909.

B.Ale.K69 3719

Alexandra Street was also the site of the YMCA, designed by the architect of the Corn Exchange which had provided the home for the first regular film shows in 1908, seen here from St Tibbs Row when demolition had revealed a new glimpse of Lloyds Bank in the background.

Culpan 4.5.1

Falcon Yard, running alongside Alexandra Street, was
named after the inn where
Elizabeth I had stayed. Later
it became a notorious slum
and was condemned in 1902.
Re-development included an
extension to the Lion Hotel
which incorporated a
covered corridor across the
street, linking new rooms
with the old.   *170/05*

Down an alley beside Heffers Bookshop stood
the imposing frontage of a solicitor's office, once
home to a surgeon. At the back it had a big bay
window which overlooked large gardens hidden
in the centre of a city.

Culpan 1.10.3

All disappeared from the map to create a building site for what had been described in 1959 as 'the biggest redevelopment scheme yet in England if we omit the blitzed cities'. Seen from the Guildhall, January 1973, are the front of Boots and shops in Petty Cury, Lloyds Bank and Great St Andrew's Church. *6663/12a*

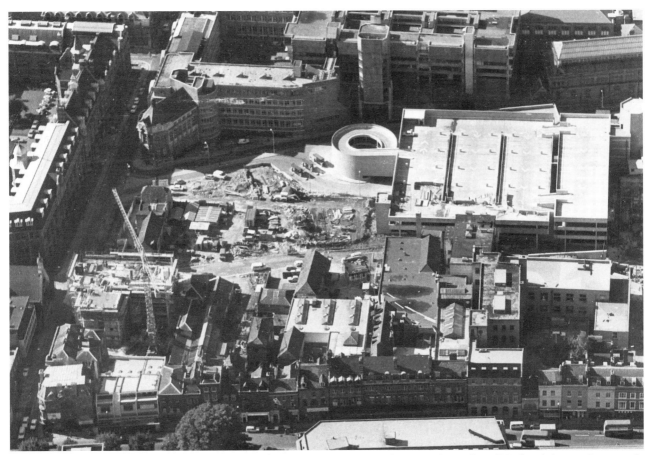

Lion Yard car-park with its spiral roadway opened in 1972 (Within 30 years the car park was demolished and the area between St Andrew's Street, Corn Exchange Street and Downing Street redeveloped as part of a 'Grand Arcade' shopping scheme). *9447/23*

The Lion Yard complex of shops, offices and a new Central Library was opened by Princess Anne in 1975. *33257511*

Not everybody approved of the scale and design of this second major change to the streetscape in 40 years – the junction of Petty Cury and Sidney Street where 1930s and 1970s buildings face each other (1983). *8238336*

More construction had taken place on the other side of Corn Exchange Street where the university rebuilt its New Museums Site, the crane seeming about to add extra spires to King's College Chapel. *D2.Mus.K7 47427*

Meanwhile to the north, Trinity College was fighting planning policies to transform derelict land on Milton Road which had been used as a tank testing ground during World War Two and once home to 850 US Army personnel into a new Science Park. *3793/25*

The university also continued its expansion to the west of the city with a new Cavendish Laboratory in 1973 and the Mullard Radio Telescope opening at Lords Bridge in 1972. Here Mayor Peter Wright is visiting in January 1973.

6805/7a

The Science Park was to link some of the scientific research within the university to commercial applications. Situated just north of the old railway line and south of the Northern bypass, the site spanned the gap between King's Hedges estate and Milton village.

Although county planning constraints still restricted the growth of heavy industry, other industrial and warehousing estates followed, as here on derelict land at Coldham's Lane, where the Coral Park trading estate was constructed on former brickworks.

202678.8

The Co-op smashed planning policies by building the Beehive in 1969, as a discount warehouse for people wishing to buy in bulk, and then opening it to everybody. It won planning inquiries to be allowed to continue and other retailers followed suit. The Co-op also refitted its Burleigh Street store, inviting BBC disc jockey Tony Blackburn to perform the reopening ceremony in November 1973 when he was mobbed by several hundred 'weeny boppers'.   *9769/30*

It was proving a difficult economic climate for Cambridge electronics firm Pye. Hit by Government delays over the introduction of colour television in the 1960s, it was taken over by Philips in 1967; in 1973 it became the first company to be granted armorial bearings, here displayed over the door at their Newmarket Road premises.   *P.Pye.K7 29981*

New arms were also granted to the new Cambridgeshire County Council, established following local government reorganisation in 1974. The county expanded its office space at Shire Hall and later went on to build a series of office blocks on the rest of its site. In the foreground the Rex Cinema closed in 1972 and was demolished in 1979.   *1311/74/7*

Not all schemes came to fruition. Proposals by De Vere in 1968 for the biggest hotel in East Anglia, almost opposite Shire Hall on Huntingdon Road, became subject of a planning wrangle.   *1380/6*

The land opposite Shire Hall lay derelict for many years until offices were built in 1979, although soon office developments were the subject of controversy between city, county and government.   *17537910*

Above and below: There were planning gains: in Bridge Street shops on the junction with Round Church Street, threatened with demolition at the start of the decade because of their poor condition – seen here in 1971 – were restored with a new development grafted on behind.   *971.32 & B.Bri.K75 42732*

College rooms in Rose Crescent – seen above in 1978 – were redeveloped as shop units in 1979. *80578 7.26 & 24478028*

Academic building continued. Here a massive new block at Queens' is under construction in 1975, echoing the Cripps Building of a decade earlier at the other end of the Backs and dwarfing the old college across the river.   *418/75/12*

Complete new colleges were built, such as Robinson on Grange Road in 1979, the gift of a reclusive millionaire, with new extensions to the University Library beyond.

25767915

To the north of the city, houses continued to spread towards the King's Hedges Road (foreground) with Lavender Road in centre, St Kilda Avenue and Campkin Road in background, 1976.   *18267614*

The house building made the north of the city virtually a new town, but with little of the facilities normally associated with places like Milton Keynes. This is Arbury Court Shopping Centre in 1979.   *325379/27*

An adventure playground for children opened in 1973 and is seen here celebrating its 16th birthday in 1989.

251089G

A youngster growing up on Arbury in 1973.

8658/10a

The lament of a lack of facilities for youth continued, although the Howard Mallet Youth Club opened in 1969, the Manor Youth Centre in 1973 and the Kelsey Kerridge Sports Hall in 1975. The latter was soon used for concerts.

Scoon 27536

Disturbances flared between town and gown, the 1971 Rag being abandoned due to violence, leading to an additional 'float', manned by the police, in the 1972 parade. Experiments in moving the date failed and the Rag seemed doomed.   *30/17 & 3359/21a*

Buskers were hit by a crack-down on street traders. One-man band Jerry Bol (seen here in 1975) was arrested for infringing new rules in August 1978.   *3666757a*

Students expressed themselves in debate. Enoch Powell, Ted Heath and David Steele at the Cambridge Union, 1979.   *13417937*

Demonstrations were also seen as a powerful means of expression. Here in 1973, one 'demo' takes place under the watchful eye of a Proctor, whose role was changed in reforms which offered students greater participation in the running of the university.

1547/75/17a

The Duke of Edinburgh became Chancellor in 1977 and took an active interest in both gown and town affairs. He is seen here in an Honorary Degree procession in 1981.

225681

In a major change of policy, women were admitted to previously all-male colleges from 1972. Soon every college was open to women, although some still excluded men.

28037821

The traditions of university life continued: *Top:* a degree day group in 1975. *Bottom:* May Balls were followed by breakfast, although here in the less than traditional setting of Waffles in June 1974.   1717/75/94 & 1487/74/24

Waffles Café off Fitzroy Street, one of the small-scale shops in the twilight romantic area of Cambridge becoming known as the Kite.
173578

Fitzroy Street showing Laurie & McConnal's store at Christmas-time. But in the cold light of economic reality the area was stagnating. Laurie's closed in 1977, blaming indecision over the redevelopment plans for the area. *P.Lau.K7 42999*

Short-term leases enabled shops to set up – as here at the Fitzroy Street-Gold Street junction – which could not afford the rents in the city centre. The leases also provided cheap accommodation for students at the Technical College and homes for the old-age pensioners still living in the houses of their birth, while other families had moved away to better houses elsewhere. It was not worth repairing property when the future of the entire area was subject to debate and buildings, once empty, were demolished, adding to the atmosphere of decay.   *B.Fit.K6 40421*

Above and opposite page:
A Kite Community Action Group was established to fight proposals to build a mammoth shopping centre. The group's name reflected the shape of the area due for redevelopment. They chose as their headquarters the Little Kettle, which had 50 years before been an old-style ironmongers when the area was alive and trading (seen here in 1939).

B.Fit.K39 15858
& 10109/16

Protest continued with concerts featuring Clive James, Michael Palin and Terry Jones in 1981 and marches like this one in January 1980.   *1158024*

The city council debated and reconsidered the Kite redevelopment scheme. Councillor John Powley is speaking in the Guildhall Council Chamber in March 1978.   *7267810*

Well, the Kite plan may be a dead duck but its a damn sight more difficult designing something the public actually like.'

Plan after plan were considered and rejected – a cartoon of April 1976 – before agreement was reached with Grosvenor Developments in 1978.   *CEN 13.4.76*

The bulldozers moved in, demolishing a wide area between Newmarket Road and the *Cambridge Evening News* offices (right), East Road where the dualling suddenly stops (left), and Burleigh Street (in background).   *3208819*

The 1980s and the '90s

The new Grafton Centre was opened by the Queen in 1984, over 30 years after it had been first suggested.   *18392*

The Grafton Centre transformed Fitzroy Street, with new shops and accommodation stretching from the old Laurie & McConnal store, now taken by Habitat.
5320933

The old Eden Baptist Chapel was retained at the entrance in a now-pedestrianised Fitzroy Street.

8398411

An enclosed arcade provided access to both specialist shops and large stores such as Debenhams and C&A, previously not represented in Cambridge. Although Presto supermarket closed in 1988, being no longer economic in a centre which was principally fashion orientated, plans were already in hand for an extension.

422907a

Mill Road continued to offer a wide range of shops on both sides of the bridge. Here is the busy city side in 1980.   *109780*

The more relaxed atmosphere across the bridge in Romsey Town – time to chat over the veg.   *8867617*

Still a relaxed atmosphere but concentrating over the fruit machines in 1986.   *3808635*

Not everybody supported all their local shops: a protest against 'The Confidential Book Shop' in July 1989.   *38428915*

Meanwhile, others expressed their anger in different ways – 1986.   *51968633*

In the city centre various large shops were in a period of change: Robert Sayle announced its intention to move to an out-of-town shopping complex, although the scheme was rejected by the Government. Another of the city's oldest shops, Joshua Taylor, closed, although the building reopened to house a range of independent traders, while its neighbour, W. Eaden Lilley, rebuilt, removing its old façade seen here in 1978 before it too ceased trading.   *172478*

Other shops closed due to three Rs – rents, rates, recession – including Bacon's tobacconists, while Bodger's outfitters disappeared from the corner of Green Street, and J.P.Gray, bookbinders, from further down (1981). *146981.9*

Christ's College refurbished its 1960s development in King Street with new shops and student accommodation, bringing a more human touch back to the street (1994).   *749947*

In 1989, Marks & Spencer won a planning appeal to open a new store in place of the Victoria Cinema on Market Hill, which was itself subject to debate with a variety of proposals to redesign the area (1993).   *4.12.93*

Above and left: After considerable debate the Corn Exchange was refurbished as a concert hall providing a venue for a variety of entertainments. Crowds on the first night in February 1986.

8.14 & 609786

A number of nightclubs were established, including Ronelles in Lion Yard. This picture shows a 14-18 disco in June 1988.*27908813*

Strawberry Fair, launched as a free pop festival in the 1970s, continued to attract a large number of pop fans. It is pictured here in 1993.
                                                                                                                            33412934

But some youngsters felt that there was a lack of facilities to party. A rave at Thakes derelict cycle shop in East Road led to disturbances in November 1985.   *51498510*

Ultimately there was a new meeting place for youth. Crowds in February 1990 at 'The Junction' which attracted a wide range of groups to a purpose-built centre off Cherry Hinton Road.   *8979020*

With the backing of the city council, South Cambridgeshire District Council, and Eastern Arts the venture proved successful attracting over 100,000 people a year. It has been joined by a cinema, and other facilities.   *73291*

'The Junction' was opened on the site of the Cattle Market (seen here in 1976). Once a major livestock sales area, it declined when the machinery market was removed to Cowley Road in 1975.   *44157612*

Both sites were chosen for a park-and-ride service seen as encouraging motorists to leave their cars on the outskirts of the city – with later suggestions for a park-and-bike scheme. Other park and ride sites have been established on the edge of the city. *44157612*

Motorists have been discouraged from driving into the centre with rigorous attacks on illegal parking, a tow-away scheme and increasingly high parking charges. *369992*

When the new Grafton Centre car-parks opened, New Square car-park closed and went back under grass. It is seen here in May 1979.

5.79

Attention focussed on Drummer Street bus station which had changed little since its original opening. Seen here in November 1978
.

40807822

Once more plans to take an extra section of Christ's Pieces were scrapped and it was redesigned, although not without controversy, the new glass waiting areas becoming too hot in summer.   *3611916*

Cambridge Railway Station, opened in 1845, was given a face lift in preparation for electric trains which made their first run in January 1987.   *31218123*

Visitors arriving by train still found the station a long distance from the sights they had come to see. Open-top buses appeared on the scene in May 1987, allowing tourists an easy way to see the sights – Silver Street in 1988.   *300488*

As tourist numbers continued to increase, several colleges closed their gates during examination periods, to minimise disruption to their students, and introduced entrance charges at other times. Blue Badge Guides were trained to lead parties around the colleges – some guiders becoming attractions in their own right. John Mellanby (who died in 1994) had pioneered such schemes in the 1950s. He is seen here guiding a group from the Richard III Society in August 1983.   *321083*

Increasing numbers of language school students also caused and experienced difficulties. These bored students are on Peas Hill, July 1988.   *327588*

Foreign students have a special problem in understanding the complexities of traffic restrictions – Trinity Street 1992.   *32349214*

Such traffic restrictions – which included the complete pedestrianisation of the central area – caused problems for shoppers and the elderly. A demonstration in February 1993.

1049939

The narrowing of various streets meant that all traffic had to proceed at cyclist's pace.

Scoon 27815

A 'Green Bike' scheme was introduced, providing cycles which people could borrow and return to designated places. Alas, most quickly disappeared and the scheme was scrapped. *71799332*

Cycleways were signposted and a new cycle bridge built. The longest of its type in Western Europe, it was opened in 1989. *60458923*

Others bridges closed and in 1981 a temporary bridge was constructed in Bridge Street to keep traffic moving.   *40548122*

While Magdalene Bridge was rebuilt in the original style (1988).   *D388856*

In 1992, Victoria Bridge was also rebuilt , having taken longer to repair than it had to construct 100 years earlier in the horse-drawn era. *Woods*

Mill Road Bridge was widened in 1980, allowing electric trains to pass underneath – and apparently Hercules aircraft to pass over, a reflection of the work at Marshalls Aerospace which won contracts converting Hercules to tankers during the Falklands War and became specialists in this and other types of aircraft. *11518445*

In the small streets off Mill Road traffic restrictions improved safety – Gwydir Street in 1982.   *107582.15*

In Cherry Hinton, traffic calming measures were introduced, although residents petitioned for the retention of a pelican crossing in 1993 and fought a long campaign for safer level-crossing gates.   *264393*

Milton Road trees, providing an attractive approach to the city, were threatened with the axe in 1993 as part of a plan to install bus lanes and an attractive floral roundabout at the junction with King's Hedges Road was replaced withtraffic lights   *170/03*

Other proposals for roads across the river and at Trumpington were also the subject of protests – like this one in June 1990 – including plans to complete the dualling of East Road.   *38559012*

On East Road, the Cambridgeshire College of Arts and Technology, founded to provide technical training, became Anglia Polytechnic University, establishing its own traditions and perhaps providing new work for gown makers.   *7066937*

The College of Further Education took on the job-related vocational courses, becoming the Cambridge Regional College with a new building on King's Hedges Road, opened by the Queen in 1993.   *5959317*

Within the old university another Royal Prince arrived – Edward, who studied at Jesus College, becoming involved with the Cambridge Youth Theatre and participating in the Rag in 1984.   *9028415*

Left: The fortunes of the Rag were revived, although not recapturing the exuberance of previous decades – a drenching for participants in Trinity Street, 1981.   *70181.33*

Right: In October 1988, Sebastian Coe and Steve Cram ran around the Great Court of Trinity College while the clock struck 12 (or rather 24 since it strikes twice, once for Trinity and once for St John's), attracting international publicity for one of those quirky things that remain associated with Cambridge and perpetuated in the film 'Chariots of Fire' – its title an allusion to the Edwardian Rag prank of commandeering a hansom cab and setting it on fire, the distraught horse dashing round and round Market Hill.   *29.10.88*

Many new college buildings were constructed, Downing New Fellows building reinterpreting the Victorian classical architecture of the main college.   *56289026a*

New buildings in Silver Street for Darwin College attracted less enthusiastic reviews. *55919323a*

New departments were opened, including the Needham Institute with its mixture of East Asian and East Anglian features standing in Chinese landscaped gardens in Sylvester Road and housing the largest collection of scientific works outside China. *56289026a*

Human and animal protesters ensured the Vet School was saved – January 1989.   *404899a*

The Judge Institute of Management Studies was established, making use of part of the Old Addenbrooke's Hospital.

7069412

Meanwhile, on the New Addenbrooke's site, which had expanded greatly since its opening in 1962, the Rosie Maternity Hospital was opened in 1983 – here looking something like a car-park (another facility the hospital needs). *3695817*

Mill Road Hospital was remodelled as Ditchburn Place sheltered accommodation and opened by the Duke of Edinburgh in 1990, providing general and special needs housing with other support to encourage development of an independent community.

41849025

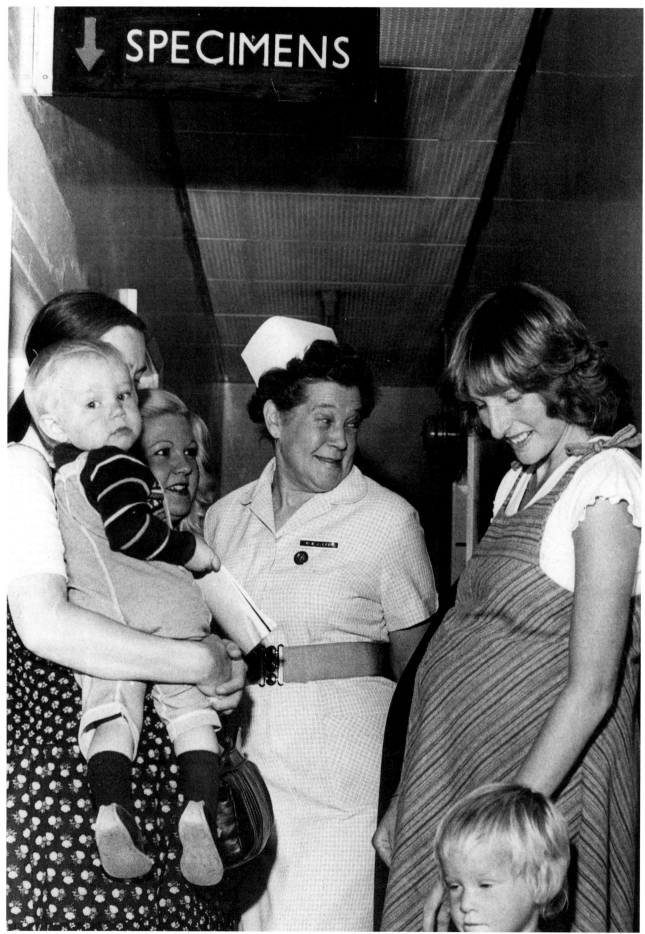

The Rosie, named by benefactor David Robinson after his mother, replaced Mill Road Hospital, where top-class maternity care had been provided in the wholly inadequate buildings of the former workhouse. Are these really specimen mums? The picture was taken in 1979.

25407932

The problems of homelessness continue, despite hostels provided by the Cyrenians, Church Army and Emmaus, with surveys indicating similar levels of poverty as existed in Victorian times.

60891 9

Older property was renovated and modernised – Darwin Drive, 1982 – although some of the 'Unity' houses erected after World War Two were described as unsellable.

3348833

The remodelling of Quayside, meanwhile, provided luxury flats on the site of the former electricity generating station.   *548191*

Additional tourist beds increased with the opening of the Holiday Inn in Downing Street in 1991.   *47719011a*

The opening of the Holiday Inn compensated for those beds lost with the closure of the Blue Boar in Trinity Street in 1986, which became student accommodation. Its sign continues to hang over the street in the 1990s. *3182928*

Downing College introduced new shops and offices into Regent Street, forming a backdrop to part of the Cambridge Festival celebrations of 1987.

3053871

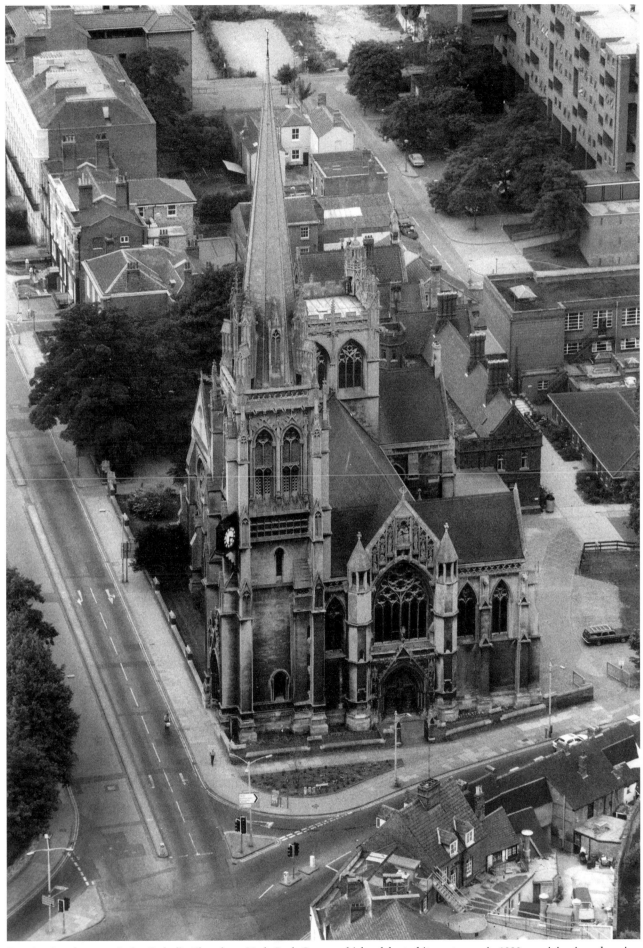

Dominating the street is the Catholic Church at Hyde Park Corner which celebrated its centenary in 1990, surviving in a changing world.

3733897a

The 'redundant' building of St Andrew the Great was used by the Greek Orthodox Church. Here is Greek Archbishop Methodios with Father Ambrosios Giakalis in December 1984.
60978418a

Various plans for the use of the former St Andrew the Great Church for a shopping area or tourist centre were discussed (here is a 1989 suggestion) until finally it reopened as a place of worship for the overflowing congregation of the Holy Sepulchre Church in 1994.   *51168*

The much-loved Eagle Inn in Bene't Street was closed for refurbishment, reopening to critical acclaim in October 1992 after four years. Similar restoration of King's Parade properties left them looking largely unchanged. *30699427*

Royal visitors continued to attract attention. Princess Diana at Cherry Hinton in August 1989.

A regular Cambridge attraction, old Snowy Farr with his menagerie of remarkable animals, a regular sight in Petty Cury raising money for Guide Dogs for the Blind. *T.D. K85 29262*

Another Cambridge 'personality' – scientist Stephen Hawking, whose brilliant mind was imprisoned in a failing body. *15.6.89*

Increased media attention came with the opening of two radio stations, BBC Radio Cambridgeshire and CNFM based in Histon, while the city's oldest newspaper, the *Cambridge Evening News,* celebrated its centenary in 1988, was named Newspaper of the Year in its class in 1994 and remains the leading local news medium into the 21st century. Former Labour leader Neil Kinnock presented the award to the paper's eleventh editor Robert Satchwell. *16.2.94*

Into 2000

When I produced the first edition of this book in 1994 I sought to speculate on the developments the Cambridge Evening News would have reported before the end of the century. The picture shows a parade of vehicles in Market Street in 1992 with the News van leading a float marked 'Recycling'. One thing that history teaches is that it will repeat itself – so could I look forward by looking back.

Shops: In earlier times the central shops existed to serve the University and closed when the students went down at the end of term. "For three months of the year Cambridge is almost a deserted city and trade dwindles to a mere trickle," the paper reported in 1922. The solution then was seen as larger stores attracting people in to the centre to shop. The 1930s saw massive redevelopment in Sidney Street and the rebuilding of much of the north side of Petty Cury. The south side was razed for the Lion Yard shopping precinct which opened in 1975. It included a multi-storey car park and magistrates court, both of which have now been demolished while the land beyond is redeveloped for a new Grand Arcade, with more shops including an expanded John Lewis on the site of the former Robert Sayles. This will compete for shoppers with the Grafton Centre, which itself is continuing to expand.

Bradwell's Court – the city's first shopping arcade – opened in 1960 and was demolished in 2006. Other shops become vacant with regularity and those that remain need to rely for their trade either on visitors or on residents journeying to the centre. The former have far more interesting reasons for visiting Cambridge than shopping, the latter are often limited to a quick visit because of high parking prices or inhibited from buying because of the difficulty of transporting purchases on buses to outlying car-parks.

But the University now no longer closes for long periods – no sooner do undergraduates move out than conferences and Summer Schools move in. Perhaps this is the future for city centre shopping after all.

Market Hill. Following a great fire in 1849 the council considered a variety of proposals for the reconstruction of Market Hill, creating a much larger, square trading area which continues to serve both town and gown with a wide range of produce and services. Plans for a new ornate central fountain to replace the one pulled down in 1953 have come to nothing and although increasing restrictions on driving and parking in the city centre have added to the problems of market traders, predictions of its demise have so far proved groundless.
28039224

Cambridge's public library service started in 1855 and for many years operated from Wheeler Street, at the back of the Guildhall. It moved to a new library in the Lion Yard redevelopment in 1975 with Lending, Children's and Music departments on the first floor, Reference Library on the second and the Cambridgeshire Collection – the source of many of these pictures – on the third. Now another redevelopment is planned which will see its closure for some 15 months, leaving the city without a central library for the first time in over 150 years. Meanwhile, its old domed building provides a home for the Tourist Information Centre.   *66129313*

Tourism: Cambridge has not sought to attract visitors, as it gets more than enough as it is. When an exhibition on the history of tourism was staged at the Guildhall in the early 1970s it included a series of panels extolling the virtues of Cambridge, which had been put together by the City Planning Department. In opening the exhibition the Mayor repeated the city's policy of not promoting visitors while standing in front of the very panels compiled to do exactly that!

Tourism is here to stay but the sheer weight of numbers causes organisational difficulties and disruption to the principal colleges on the main tourist trail. Restrictions have been imposed during sensitive examination times and several colleges have introduced charges, using some of the income to employ staff in gowns to manage the crowds. These could themselves become part of the attraction of Cambridge and provide employment for impoverished students.

At the same time as restricting tourists many colleges now welcome International Summer Schools and actively promote themselves as conference venues with purposely-designed facilities. Already some college rooms are rented to visitors during summer months and soon there might be package holidays taking advantage of the proximity of Stansted airport, echoing the railwaymen who in 1912 suggested advertising Cambridge like a seaside town to encourage visitors during the Long Vacation. Some would claim that with global warming and rising sea levels Cambridge might one day itself be once more surrounded by water – although not perhaps to the extreme that the *Cambridge Evening News* photographer envisaged in 1993! *525593*

Transport: Cambridge has been struggling with the motor vehicle for generations. The first car was owned by an undergraduate – C.S.Rolls – and the university imposed restrictions on its students' cars in the 1920s. Traffic restrictions have included one-way streets and the total banning of all vehicles in some areas at some times enforced by rising bollards that have speared several tourists' cars and left them with an unforgettable memory of their visit.

Parking provision has been increased by the creation of car parks and park-and-ride sites and reduced by the banning of on-street parking. Traffic meters have been replaced by pay-and-display machines, allowing tourists to park along the Backs next to the sights they have come to see but with no time to get into the centre for shopping.

Other plans have included a tunnel below Queens' Road – illustrated by the Cambridge Evening News photographers in 1981. This has not yet materialised but who can predict the planners' solutions of the future?   *940709*

Entertainment: People have always complained that there was insufficient entertainment or recreation in Cambridge, although the university has many sporting facilities. Ice-skating was popular on the flooded commons in the 1890s and proposals for a rink were promoted in the 1970s and 1980s. Greyhound racing tracks were established off Arbury and Cherry Hinton Roads in the 1920s and on Milton Road in the 1960s until it closed in 1983. A municipal golf course was being canvassed in 1912, a ten-pin bowling alley flourished for a while in the 1960s and a water-polo team in 1910. Swimming pools have been fought for and agonised over, cricket matches played on Parker's Piece. Football stadiums were established on Milton Road and Newmarket Road (shown in 1994) but the future of each is now uncertain and alternatives are being considered. *24549432*

New houses continue to be built as more and more people seek to make their homes in the area. Already the former village of Trumpington and Cherry Hinton have seen massive new development as seen in this photograph taken in 1992 with Fulbourn Road in foreground, Malletts Road, Leete Road and Bridgwell Road centre. Now the land between King's Hedges Road and the A14, Northern Bypass, is being transformed from allotments to shops and accommodation. But whatever happens people will always wish to visit and make their home in this most special part of England, each with their own personal 'Images of Cambridge' *70269216*

Index